Benjamin Franklin

American Statesman, Scientist, and Writer

Colonial Leaders

Lord Baltimore *English Politician and Colonist*

Benjamin Banneker *American Mathematician and Astronomer*

William Bradford *Governor of Plymouth Colony*

Benjamin Franklin *American Statesman, Scientist, and Writer*

Anne Hutchinson *Religious Leader*

Cotton Mather *Author, Clergyman, and Scholar*

William Penn *Founder of Democracy*

John Smith *English Explorer and Colonist*

Miles Standish *Plymouth Colony Leader*

Peter Stuyvesant *Dutch Military Leader*

Revolutionary War Leaders

Benedict Arnold *Traitor to the Cause*

Nathan Hale *Revolutionary Hero*

Alexander Hamilton *First U.S. Secretary of the Treasury*

Patrick Henry *American Statesman and Speaker*

Thomas Jefferson *Author of the Declaration of Independence*

John Paul Jones *Father of the U.S. Navy*

Thomas Paine *Political Writer*

Paul Revere *American Patriot*

Betsy Ross *American Patriot*

George Washington *First U.S. President*

Colonial Leaders

Benjamin Franklin

American Statesman, Scientist, and Writer

Bruce & Becky Durost Fish

Arthur M. Schlesinger, jr.
Senior Consulting Editor

Chelsea House Publishers

Philadelphia

CHELSEA HOUSE PUBLISHERS
Editor in Chief Stephen Reginald
Production Manager Pamela Loos
Director of Photography Judy L. Hasday
Art Director Sara Davis
Managing Editor James D. Gallagher

Staff for *BENJAMIN FRANKLIN*
Project Editor Anne Hill
Project Editor/Publishing Coordinator Jim McAvoy
Contributing Editor Amy Handy
Associate Art Director Takeshi Takahashi
Series Design Keith Trego
Digital Designer Robert Gerson

The Chelsea House World Wide Web Address
is http://www.chelseahouse.com

3 5 7 9 8 6 4 2

Library of Congress Cataloging-in-Publication Data

Fish, Bruce
Benjamin Franklin / by Bruce and Becky Durost Fish.
    p. cm. — (Colonial leaders)
Includes bibliographical references (p.   ) and index.
Summary: A biography of the well known American statesman,
inventor, printer, and author of "Poor Richard's Almanacks."
ISBN 0-7910-5347-4 (HC) 0-7910-5690-2 (PB)
1. Franklin, Benjamin, 1706-1790 Juvenile literature.   2. Statesmen—United
States Biography Juvenile literature.   3. Inventors—United States Biography Juve-
nile literature.   4. Scientists—United States Biography Juvenile literature.
5. Printers—United States Biography Juvenile literature.
[1. Franklin, Benjamin, 1706-1790. 2. Statesmen. 3. Printers. 4. Scientists.]
I. Fish, Becky Durost. II. Title. III. Series.
E302.6.F8F52 1999
973.3'092—dc21
[B]
                                                                    99-15210
                                                                        CIP

Thank you to John Alviti, Curator of the Franklin Institute and Science Museum,
for his assistance in acquiring pictures for this book.

Publisher's Note: In Colonial and Revolutionary War America, there were no standard rules for spelling, punctuation, capitalization, or grammar. Some of the quotations that appear in the Colonial Leaders and Revolutionary War Leaders series come from original documents and letters written during this time in history. Original quotations reflect writing inconsistencies of the period.

Contents

In a time long before there was radio, television, or the Internet, people had to find news and entertainment in other ways. They often bought printed sheets of news or poems from street sellers. Young Ben sold copies of his ballad *The Lighthouse Tragedy* this way.

A Smart Young Man

An excited group of children waited for news. They didn't notice how cold it was that Sunday. Their mother was about to have a baby. It was January 17, 1706.

A cry rang out. The Franklin family had a new baby brother. His parents named him Benjamin. Ben was his parents' eighth child.

Ben Franklin grew up in a busy home. He had many brothers and sisters. Some of them were children of his father's first wife. She died long before Ben was born. Thirteen children often gathered around the dinner table.

The Franklins lived in a small, rented house in

Benjamin Franklin was born in this house on Milk Street in Boston, across from the old South Church. He was the family's eighth child.

Boston. Ben's father made candles and soap. He worked hard and treated people fairly. Ben's mother loved to read. Ben learned how to read when he was three or four years old. Probably his mother taught him.

When Ben was six years old, the family bought a house. His father's shop was in part of the house. It was the perfect place for selling candles and soap. A large open fireplace heated the house. Ben's mother cooked food in the fireplace.

The children gathered and chopped wood for the fire. They swept up ash from the fire and carried it outside. Dirt, smoke, soot, and bugs made the house hard to keep clean. The children carried buckets of water to the house. They used it for cooking, cleaning, and drinking. Dirty water was dumped outside.

Ben loved being outdoors. He taught himself how to swim, and he rowed and sailed in small boats. Sometimes, when Ben wasn't doing chores, he explored Boston. Boston was an important city. It was almost completely surrounded by water, and a huge dock ran about 1000 feet out into the **harbor.** It was called the Long Wharf. The largest sailing ships in the world tied up next to it. Men carried **cargo** off the ships.

Boston has been a major city ever since Colonial times. Here colonists stand along the harbor, perhaps waiting for cargo from the ships.

Ben watched people and ships at Boston Harbor. The Long Wharf was just one of the exciting places that Ben and his friends explored. They visited sail lofts. Workers cut huge pieces of canvas for sails, and they sewed the sails with long steel needles. Shops sold telescopes, brass bells, and tools that guided ships across the ocean.

Ben was smarter than most of his friends. Smart boys were trained for jobs in the church,

Today Boston remains an important port city, though it looks very different than it did when young Ben explored it.

medicine, and teaching. Mr. Franklin decided Ben should be a pastor.

In the fall of 1714 Ben entered the Boston Latin School. He was eight years old. Ben learned to read, write, and speak Latin. He learned to read Greek. The teachers also taught math. These lessons were the first step to becoming a pastor.

Ben learned things quickly. The teachers promoted him faster than the other students. It was like going from second grade to sixth grade in one year.

But there was a problem. Ben wasn't excited about church and praying. Ben's father said long prayers before and after every meal. Ben got bored.

One day the Franklins fixed some food to eat during the winter. They put it in a big wooden cask. Ben said, "I think, Father, if you were to say *Grace* over the whole cask–once for all–it would be a vast *saving of time.*"

Ben's father thought about what Ben said. He decided that Ben wouldn't make a good pastor. After one year, Ben stopped going to the Latin School.

The next year, Ben went to George Brownell's writing school. Here Ben learned more about reading, writing, and math.

Now Ben needed to learn a job. The ten-year-old boy became an **apprentice** for his father. Ben worked 12 to 14 hours a day, six days a week. Ben cut the wicks for the candles.

Ben always loved books, so when he was 12 he became an apprentice in the print shop of his brother James.

He filled the molds that shaped the candles. He helped customers.

Ben did not like this work. His father figured that Ben would be better off doing something else. Since Ben was so interested in books, Mr. Franklin thought he might like printing. He apprenticed Ben to James Franklin. James was

Ben's 21-year-old brother. Ben was 12 years old.

Ben was a great help to James. He worked hard. He was very strong. Ben could already read, write, and do simple math. Most apprentices had to be taught these skills.

Printing in Ben Franklin's day was a slow process. Everything was done by hand. Each letter, punctuation mark, and even the spaces between words was formed by an individual piece of type. Those pieces were put together by hand to make up a page. Usually, four pages were printed together on a single sheet of paper. Two people couldn't aprint more than 16 pages in a minute.

The print shop had a small library. Ben loved reading these books. One of the shop's customers owned many books. The man let Ben borrow them.

Ben started writing for James. In November 1718 the keeper of Boston's lighthouse drowned. His wife, daughter, and two other people also died. Ben wrote a poem called *The Lighthouse Tragedy.* James printed it, and Ben sold it on the streets of Boston. They sold many copies.

In August 1721 James Franklin began to publish a weekly newspaper, the *New-England Courant.*

James's paper carried both news and funny stories.

Smallpox broke out in Boston that summer. A powerful man in Boston named Cotton Mather thought he knew how to keep people from dying. He wanted people to try new shots. These shots gave people a mild form of smallpox. Many people thought that the shots were stupid and dangerous. James's paper argued against the shots. This helped James sell a lot of newspapers. It also made Cotton Mather and the other leaders of Boston very angry.

Many people wrote for James's paper. They didn't want their names known. So they made up funny names to use. Some of the names were Fanny Mournful, Homespun Jack, and Tabitha Talkative.

Ben worked for James for four years. He wanted to write about life in Boston. Ben thought James wouldn't print his stories because he was young. So Ben made up a name for himself. It was Silence Dogood.

Silence Dogood was supposed to be a widow

Ben learned all about the printing trade when he worked for James, and he also wrote for his brother's newspaper.

living near Boston. She wrote letters for James's newspaper. The letters were very funny and also very wise. On April 2, 1722, the first Silence

Dogood letter was published in James's paper. People rushed to buy newspapers that had letters from Silence.

Readers liked Silence, but James still had problems. The leaders of Boston were still angry with him. That summer, they put James in prison for a month. Ben ran the newspaper.

By the beginning of 1723 the leaders ordered James to stop running the paper. James didn't want to go to prison again. But he needed to sell the paper to make money. So James put Ben in charge of the paper. That way James wasn't running the paper, but he could still sell it.

Ben had his own ideas for the paper. He and James didn't agree. Ben and James argued about the paper for months.

Ben was very unhappy. He decided he should live somewhere else. He would run away. A friend helped Ben sneak onto a ship bound for New York City. The ship set sail near the end of September. Ben was starting a great adventure.

Ben Franklin lived in many places
throughout his life. One place he is
particularly associated with is Philadelphia,
where he first went to work for a printer
when he was 17. This photograph shows
the modern city of Philadelphia, a city
that Ben's inventive mind helped to shape
in Colonial times.

On His Own

At first, everything went well for Ben. It took only three days for the ship to reach New York City. Then everything started going wrong.

Ben hoped to get a job with a printer named William Bradford in New York. But Mr. Bradford didn't have enough work even to keep himself busy. He couldn't hire another printer. He told Ben to go to Philadelphia. Mr. Bradford's son lived in that city. He might be able to give Ben work.

Ben took a small boat from New York to New Jersey. A storm came up and pushed the boat back to Long Island. It took more than 30 hours to get to New Jersey.

Then Ben had to walk 50 miles to find a boat going to Philadelphia. Rain started falling. Soon Ben was soaked through.

Ben finally reached Philadelphia on a Sunday morning in October. His clothes were wet and dirty. The pockets stuck out. They were stuffed with Ben's extra shirts and socks. He was tired and hungry. And he had very little money. But Ben's luck was about to change.

The next day Ben cleaned himself up. Then he went to visit Mr. Bradford's son. The son didn't have a job for Ben. He suggested that Ben see another printer, Samuel Keimer.

Mr. Keimer offered Ben a job. He also arranged for Ben to rent a room at the Read house.

Mr. Read had a daughter named Deborah. Ben liked Deborah. They spent a lot of time together. They talked about getting married, but Deborah's mother thought she was too young.

Ben did very well at his job. He was a better printer than his boss. Ben made lots of friends.

They liked his jokes, and they admired how hard he worked.

Early the next year, Ben got a letter from his sister's husband. It said that Ben's parents were worried about him. Ben sent a letter back that told why he had left Boston. The letter reached Ben's brother-in-law while the governor of Pennsylvania was visiting him. Governor Keith liked the way Ben wrote.

When the governor got back to Philadelphia, he stopped by Mr. Keimer's print shop. Mr. Keimer was surprised when Governor Keith asked to speak to Ben. Governors didn't usually talk to 18-year-old printers.

Governor Keith wanted Ben to start his own printing shop. He told Ben to ask his father to help him set up a shop. Ben's father thought that his son was too young. He wouldn't give Ben the money he needed.

Then the governor offered to lend Ben the money. Ben was very excited. Governor Keith made plans for Ben to sail to England. There,

This view of the River Thames in London is probably something like what Ben saw when he arrived in England on Christmas Eve of 1724.

Ben could buy the printing press and other things he needed.

On November 5, 1724, Ben left Philadelphia on the *London Hope.* It was his first trip across the Atlantic Ocean. For seven weeks, the small ship hit one storm after another. Huge waves tossed it up and down. And the food was even worse than the weather. They ate salted, dried meat, and hard biscuits.

Everyone on ship was happy to see land. The ship reached England on Christmas Eve. Ben waited for the mail bags to be opened. He was supposed to get letters from Governor Keith to help him buy the things he needed. But the letters weren't there.

Ben had met a man named Thomas Denham on the ship. Mr. Denham told Ben that the governor wasn't good at keeping his promises. Now Ben was in a strange country. He had no money. He couldn't get home. He needed to find a job.

Shortly after Christmas, Ben got a job as a printer. He learned more things about printing.

Some printers had to quit working. This was because they worked with lead type. Their hands got covered with lead. If they didn't wash their hands before meals, the lead got into their food. The lead made them very sick. Ben was careful to wash his hands.

A couple of years later, Mr. Denham visited Ben. Mr. Denham was going to start a new business in Philadelphia. He wanted Ben to work for him. Ben would copy his letters. He would keep track of how money was spent. He would travel.

Ben took the job. On July 23, 1726, he left England. It was another long trip. One night Ben saw a rainbow caused by moonlight. He watched dolphins swim beside the ship. He saw an **eclipse** of the sun and an eclipse of the moon. On October 11 Ben finally reached America.

At first Ben was very busy in his new job. Then Mr. Denham and Ben got very sick. Mr. Denham died.

Ben went back to work as a printer. He got a job with his old boss, Mr. Keimer. Hugh Meredith, a young man who worked at the shop, became Ben's good friend.

Both Hugh and Ben knew that Mr. Keimer didn't like having Ben around. Ben was a much better printer than Mr. Keimer. Many people liked Ben more than they liked his boss.

Hugh's father was rich. Mr. Meredith offered to help Ben and Hugh start their own printing shop. They ordered a printing press and type

One of Ben's jobs as a printer was to print paper currency. Today we can see his portrait on the 100-dollar bill.

from England. Hugh and Ben were careful not to let Mr. Keimer know about their plans.

During the fall of 1727 Ben started a club for young men. It was called the Junto. The members met every Friday night to debate important issues. They tried to think of things they could do to make life in Philadelphia better.

At about this time, Mr. Keimer got a job printing money for New Jersey. The job was very hard and only Ben could do it. He built a special press to print the money. The people from New Jersey liked Ben a lot. They invited him to parties, where he met rich and powerful people.

It took three months to print all the money. By that time, the press for Ben and Hugh's shop had arrived from England. They quit working for Mr. Keimer.

> "When I was a boy, I made two oval pallets, each about ten inches long, and six broad, with a hole for the thumb, in order to retain it fast in the palm of my hand. They much resembled a painter's pallets. In swimming I pushed the edges of these forward, and I struck the water with their flat surfaces as I drew them back. I remember I swam faster by means of these pallets, but they fatigued my wrists."

People were debating whether Pennsylvania should begin using paper money. Ben wrote an article supporting the idea. Soon the Assembly voted to use paper money. Ben and Hugh got the job of printing the money. This was a big job and it helped their business become a success.

Ben wanted their business to become even bigger. He thought Philadelphia needed a good newspaper. Philadelphia already had two papers, but Ben didn't like either of them. One of them was printed by his old boss, Mr. Keimer.

Mr. Keimer's business was not doing well, so he offered to sell his paper to Ben. In 1729 Ben bought the *Pennsylvania Gazette.* The paper was full of news, but Ben added ideas to make people's lives better. He printed funny stories.

The next year, Ben bought Hugh's part of their business. He also started a paper mill. That way he wouldn't have to buy as much paper from other people.

Ben had many friends. Some of them had put him in contact with the Read family again. On September 1, 1730, Ben married Deborah Read. He was 24 years old. He had a growing business and a family. And he had big plans for the future.

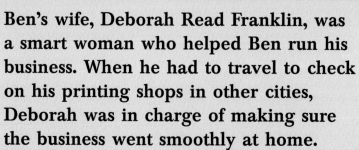

Ben's wife, Deborah Read Franklin, was
a smart woman who helped Ben run his
business. When he had to travel to check
on his printing shops in other cities,
Deborah was in charge of making sure
the business went smoothly at home.

Ben Makes Changes

Life settled down for Ben and Deborah. Ben ran his printing office out of one part of their home. Deborah was busy raising Ben's son, William.

Sometimes their house got crowded. Deborah's mother lived with them, and Deborah's brother and sister sometimes visited for weeks. The boy who worked at the shop lived with them also.

Ben was very busy. He did more than print. He sold iron stoves and cakes of soap, quill pens and ink and paper, cheese and books and tea. He also loaned money to poor people.

Ben loved reading. He wanted to read more books and he wanted others to be able to read more. So in 1732 Ben helped start a library.

On October 20 of that year, Ben and Deborah had a son whom they named Francis Folger Franklin. The family called him "young Franky." Ben loved having another child in his family.

That fall, Ben worked on a new project. He wanted to publish an **almanac**, a book with a calendar for the year that also told what the weather would be like, and listed the dates of fairs and the addresses of inns.

Ben's almanac was different from other almanacs. It had many jokes and wise sayings. He chose sayings that ordinary people would like. "Fish and visitors smell in three days," Ben wrote. "When the well's dry, we know the worth of water."

Some of Ben's sayings came from books, others he made himself. He named his almanac *Poor Richard's Almanac.* It was very popular all over the colonies. He published a new almanac every year.

Ben liked to do many things at the same time.

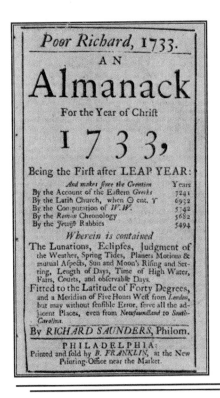

In Colonial times people checked the almanac for information on the weather and other subjects. Ben published an almanac that was also filled with clever sayings. This is the title page of the very first issue.

The next year he started learning languages. He read French, Spanish, Italian, and German.

Ben left Deborah in charge of his business so he could take a trip to New England for several weeks. He visited his family in Boston. He hadn't seen his brother James since he ran away. James was sick and told Ben that he was dying. Ben promised to look after James's son. Ben thought that this would help make up for running away.

Ben's sons were now four and two years old. Ben wanted them to start learning reading, writing, and math, so he hired a teacher to live with them and teach them. Then when Franky was four years old, he caught smallpox. Ben and Deborah did everything they could to help Franky get better, but nothing worked. Young Franky died on November 21, 1736. Ben and Deborah were terribly sad.

Ben kept on working. He wanted to make his city a better place to live. Fire was a big problem in Philadelphia. Ben printed warnings in his newspaper, telling people that they should be careful when they carried burning coals from the fireplace to their bedrooms, and that they should get their chimneys cleaned.

In Franklin's time the only way people had to heat their houses was the fireplace. But most of the heat from fireplaces went up the chimney. Ben Franklin wanted that heat to stay in the house. In 1742 he built a new stove. It held the hot air much longer than the fireplace did. This gave more time for the heat to pass into the room. Ben's stove also heated cold air from outside and sent the warm air into the house. His stove is still used today.

Yet no matter how careful people were, houses still caught on fire, and the fires spread quickly from one house to another. Ben said that the city should form a fire department. People agreed. They certainly didn't want their houses burning down.

Thirty men offered to fight fires for free. A few weeks after Franky died, Ben started the new fire company. More men offered to fight fires. Soon the city was known for how quickly its fires got put out.

Ben also worked to get better police. The men who guarded the city at night were often drunk. Widows living alone in small houses had to pay as much for the guards as men who owned large businesses. Ben helped change the system so it would be fair. The city hired and trained night watchmen.

Ben was named clerk of the Pennsylvania Assembly, which made the laws for Pennsylvania. This was Ben's first job in politics. He helped write the laws. He liked being able to get things

Ben and Deborah set up their home and business along High Street in Philadelphia. Later Ben put a post office in his shop.

done. He made friends with many important men.

Ben was happiest when he was very busy, so he wanted still more work to do. In 1737 he became postmaster of Philadelphia. The mail route in the **colonies** stretched from Boston to Charleston, South Carolina. All the mail went through Philadelphia. Ships brought more mail to Philadelphia.

The post office took up a corner of Ben's shop. Ben sorted through bags of mail. Letters for people in Philadelphia stayed in his shop. He sent the rest of the mail on its way.

People had to go to Ben's shop to pick up their mail. Most people didn't get many letters, so they didn't check for mail very often. A letter could sit in Ben's shop for days. Ben wanted people to get their mail faster so in his newspaper he printed a list of people who had received mail.

Ben was 31 years old. He had a wife and son. He had a good business. And he was busy making Philadelphia a better place for people to live. But there were many more things Ben was about to do.

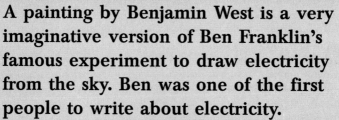

A painting by Benjamin West is a very imaginative version of Ben Franklin's famous experiment to draw electricity from the sky. Ben was one of the first people to write about electricity.

Ben Becomes Famous

Ben always looked for new things to do. He printed the first medical book and the first novel in America. One day Ben thought about printing a newspaper in German since many Germans lived around Philadelphia. Ben wasn't sure that enough people would buy a German newspaper. If the paper didn't sell well, it would cost too much to print. Ben didn't want to lose money. Ben printed one issue of the paper. He told readers that he needed 300 orders for the paper. If not, he would stop printing it. By the next issue, he had received only 50 orders. That was the end of the German newspaper. Ben was always careful about how he ran his business.

Ben liked science. He used it to make many things work better. One thing he wanted to improve was the way people kept their homes warm in the winter. It was too hot near the big fireplaces and it was very cold near the doors and windows. Ben noticed that most of the heat from the fires went right up the chimneys. He wanted to find a way to keep more heat in the houses, a way that would also use less firewood, to save people money and to keep too many trees from being cut down.

He built a special fireplace from cast iron. It spread warm air through a house and it didn't need as much wood. Ben's fireplace is still used. It's called the Franklin stove. Ben could have earned a lot of money selling his fireplace. But he didn't, because he believed that inventions should be shared freely with other people.

Ben was always looking for new ideas. He read the newspapers that came in the mail. People in other colonies were trying to figure out how things worked. They could learn faster if they shared their ideas. Ben decided to start a Philosophical Society. Members would write to each other about their ideas. Ben wrote about the Franklin stove in the group's paper.

Ben also started a school. He wanted children to learn. The school became the University of Pennsylvania.

Ben still missed young Franky. Then in 1743 Deborah told Ben some good news. They were going to have another baby. Sarah Franklin was born on September 11. Ben called her Sally.

Ben wanted to give William and Sally everything they needed. He worked harder than ever. His business grew. He owned printing shops in Boston and other cities. Deborah took care of the business at home when Ben traveled to check on his other businesses.

During a trip in 1746 Ben met a man who was working with electricity. People were just starting to learn about electricity. Ben began running his own tests. Over the next few years, he worked on electricity. He chose names to describe things

Ben and his son flew a kite in a storm and waited to see if the lightning would travel down to the key tied onto the kite string.

about electricity. Ben was the first person to write about positive and negative charges.

Many people saw that lightning and electricity were like each other. But no one had proved that lightning was made of electricity. Ben wanted to see if it was true, so in June 1752 he did an **experiment** with a kite. The day was stormy. Ben and his son, William, went to a field. They flew a kite. They tied a key to the end of the kite's string. If lightning was electric, it would travel down the string to the key. A spark would jump from the key to a finger held near it.

William and Ben waited. The wind blew. Clouds filled the sky. There was no lightning. They waited some more. Still no lightning. Ben was ready to give up. Finally lightning flashed. Ben noticed that the threads on the kite string were standing straight up. He put his finger near the key. A spark flew through the air between the key and Ben's finger. An electric charge from the lightning had traveled down the kite string to the key. Ben had proved that lightning was electric.

This was exciting news. Ben became famous in America and Europe. He told people how to use lightning rods to protect homes and barns

Franklin invented the electrostatic machine in 1745 and used it to discover principles of electricity.

from lightning. Ben also said that lightning rods could be used on ships.

Ben's idea worked. The king of France sent Ben a thank-you letter. Important science societies in England and France asked Ben to join them. He was the first American given that honor.

Ben liked working with electricity. He liked sharing ideas with people. But problems with England and France were going to change his life.

France and England had been at war for years. In 1747 French raiders sailed up the Delaware River. They got within 20 miles of Philadelphia. People were scared. Something had to be done. They wanted the government to create a **militia,** a type of army.

But there was a problem. The Penn family had settled Pennsylvania. When Pennsylvania was made an English colony, the Penn family was told it didn't have to pay taxes. The Penns could also turn down any law the Assembly of Pennsylvania passed. The Penn family and the Assembly didn't agree with each other. Important things didn't get done.

The Penn family were Quakers. Quakers didn't believe in fighting wars. So the Penn family turned down any law that would form a militia.

Ben had been clerk of the Assembly for many years. He knew Pennsylvania needed protection. He suggested that they make a volunteer militia. That way Quakers would not be forced to fight. The Assembly and the Penn family agreed. The people were protected. Then the members of the militia went home.

Ben's work with government was just starting. He would spend more time working on the problems with England and France than on anything else.

Photography was not developed for about a hundred years after Franklin's time, so people depended on portrait painters to preserve images of themselves. Artist David Martin created this wonderful picture of Ben in London in 1767.

A Voice for the Colonies

A group of Indians lived north of Pennsylvania. The French lived north of the Indians. The French made life hard for their enemies. In 1753 the Indians asked Pennsylvania for help. They wanted Pennsylvania to protect them from the French. If Pennsylvania didn't help them, the Indians would probably become friends with the French.

That would be a problem for Pennsylvania. The French could then attack the English colony with the help of the Indians.

Ben was asked to go with a group of men to talk with the Indian leaders. It was the first time Ben had worked on a **treaty**. They talked about buying things from each other. They talked about helping each other against the French. The men from Pennsylvania and the Indian leaders agreed on a treaty.

Ben wanted to work on other treaties. But he had a new job. He was deputy postmaster general of North America. The mail service between the colonies was slow. Ben visited post offices all over the colonies. He watched how they worked. He came up with ideas to move the mail more quickly.

Ben also learned about the other colonies. They all had problems with the French. The wars between France and England spread to the colonies in America.

It cost a lot of money to fight a war. Many men and boys died in the battles. England asked the colonies to pay for fighting the wars.

Ben thought the colonies should work together. The leaders from some of the colonies held a meeting. Ben said they should ask England to

Thomas Jefferson gave Ben this odometer when he was postmaster general to measure the distance of postal routes.

have a leader over all the colonies. People from each of the colonies could meet and help solve the colonies' problems.

The idea was voted down. The leaders of the colonies thought the plan would take away their power. They wouldn't be in charge of everything that happened in their colonies. England didn't like the idea either. The government was afraid it would make the colonies too strong.

During the next year, Ben visited many post offices. Then the French began attacking English colonies. They got some Indians to help them. People living on the edge of Pennsylvania were being killed.

Pennsylvania still didn't have a paid army. It needed more than a volunteer militia. The leaders kept arguing over how to do this.

People got tired of waiting for help. They brought a wagon to the place where the leaders were meeting. In the wagon were the bodies of a family that had been killed by the French and the Indians. The leaders knew they had to do something.

Ben helped get a law passed that would create a paid army. But the colony still needed to raise money so that it could pay the soldiers.

The Penn family was the richest family in Pennsylvania. But they didn't pay any taxes. The rest of the people in Pennsylvania couldn't afford to give all the money that was needed for an army.

The leaders argued over what to do. The people got very upset. The leaders managed to get some money and send out an army. But they needed a better system.

They sent Ben to England. They wanted him to ask the government to change the rules for Pennsylvania, so it would be run by the king instead of by the Penn family. Then they would be able to tax the Penns.

In the middle of June 1757 Ben left for England. He wrote a letter to his wife. He told her how glad he was that he could trust her to run their businesses.

The trip was risky. A few times, the captain thought he saw French ships. French ships would attack their English ship. The captain changed directions so that his ship wouldn't be seen. Then the ship reached the English Channel, which flows between England and France. The captain sailed the ship at night. Sailing at night was dangerous, but the captain thought it would be more dangerous to sail during the day and be seen by the French. One night the ship almost smashed into some rocks.

Finally, the ship landed in England. Everyone was happy to be safe. On July 26 Ben took a coach to the big city of London.

Ben was famous for his work with electricity. Many people wanted to meet him. But Ben had work to do. Changing the law would not be easy. The Penn family had many powerful friends. The Penns didn't want to lose their power. They didn't want to pay taxes.

Five years passed. Ben still hadn't gotten the law changed. Some people in Pennsylvania complained. They thought Ben was wasting his time. And Ben missed his home. He decided to travel back to America. Then he could answer his **critics** in person.

In August 1762 Ben sailed from England. The ship didn't reach America until November. Good news waited for Ben. England and France had signed a peace treaty. Ben's son, William, had been named governor of New Jersey.

Ben stayed in America for two years. He worked to make the post offices better.

The English Quaker William Penn founded Philadelphia in the 17th century. He is seen here meeting peacefully with Indians from that area but by Franklin's time the Penn family considered many Indians to be enemies.

He also got more upset at the Penn family. After the war between France and England, most of the Indians went back to living in peace. A few Indians kept attacking white settlers. Governor Penn offered money for the scalps of Indians. He didn't care if the Indians who got killed were guilty. Many peaceful Indians were killed.

Ben wasn't the only person upset by this. Many of Pennsylvania's leaders got very angry, and they asked Ben to go back to England. The first thing they wanted Ben to do was to try again to have Pennsylvania run by the king instead of the Penn family. But they wanted Ben to do something else as well.

The war with France had cost lots of money. The leaders were afraid that King George would try to pay for the war by taxing people in America. They asked Ben to fight against more taxes.

On November 7, 1764, Ben sailed for England. It was an awful trip. The ship traveled through many storms. Crashing waves broke parts of the ship. The food tasted terrible.

By the time they reached England, Ben was very sick. It took him weeks to get better. Then he was ready for action.

In 1765 the English government passed the Stamp Act. It made people in America pay a tax for any paper they bought. Ben argued against the tax. People would be angry. They didn't have a say in making the laws about the new tax. But even Ben was surprised at how angry the people in America became.

Mobs of people filled the streets. People stopped buying things that came from England. They attacked some of the people hired to collect the taxes. They burned down some of their houses. The other tax collectors were afraid. They knew that if they didn't quit their jobs, their homes might be burned next. They might even be killed.

The Penn family saw a chance to get back at Ben. They started spreading the story that Ben

Citizens of Boston protest the enactment of the Stamp Act by British Parliament in 1765.

had written the Stamp Act. Some people believed this story. They said they would burn down Ben's home in Philadelphia.

Ben's wife, Deborah, was brave. She stayed

in their house. Ben's friends finally convinced people that the story wasn't true.

The English government asked Ben to explain why Americans were so angry. He answered their questions. They asked him if Americans would pay the taxes. Ben said that this would only happen if someone held a gun to the people. The English decided to end the Stamp Act.

Ben knew that this was not the end of the problems between England and America. He stayed in England for nine more years. He wrote articles that told why Americans were so angry. He worked to change the way England treated America. But things just got worse.

Americans threw crates of tea into Boston Harbor. This cost the tea company lots of money. Ben offered to pay for the tea if England would change the way it treated America. The government refused.

Ben couldn't help America by staying in England. He made plans to leave. Then Ben got a

To protest their unfair treatment by the
English government, some Colonists disguised
themselves as Indians and threw tea from
British ships into the water.

letter from his son. Deborah had died. Because of his work in England, Ben hadn't seen his wife for many years. Now he would never see her again.

On March 21, 1775, Ben sailed from England. He knew that life in America would be different from what it used to be. But when he landed Ben was surprised by how many changes there were.

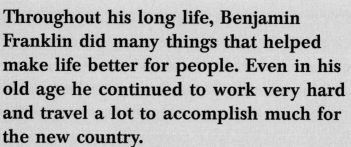

Throughout his long life, Benjamin
Franklin did many things that helped
make life better for people. Even in his
old age he continued to work very hard
and travel a lot to accomplish much for
the new country.

A New Nation

Ben returned to Philadelphia on May 5, 1775. There was bad news. Battles were taking place outside Boston. In April British soldiers had fought with Americans. No one knew who fired the first shot. People on both sides had been killed. Everyone was very upset.

The leaders of Pennsylvania asked Ben to speak for the state. Meetings took place in Philadelphia. People from all the colonies were trying to decide what to do about the fighting.

Ben was 69 years old. He was in the meetings by six o'clock each morning. He sat through meetings all day. He talked with people until late at night.

Ben was also sad. His son, William, was still governor of New Jersey. Ben told his son to stop working for the king. William refused. War with England was coming. Ben was afraid that his son would be put in prison. William might get killed. Anyone who served the king would be in danger.

The leaders thought it would help to have Canada fight against England. They sent some men to get Canada to join them. In March 1776 Ben and three other men left Philadelphia.

The trip was hard. It took two weeks to get to New York. Then they sailed up the Hudson River. Storms tore their sails.

Finally they landed in Albany, New York. Here the men took a road to Lake George. The ice that covered the lake was breaking up. Huge chunks of ice smashed against any boat in the water. Ben and his friends had to walk around the lake.

It was cold, muddy, and snowy. Ben got a fur hat to keep warm. They finally reached Montreal, Canada, on April 29. They were very tired. Ben was sick. He had huge sores on his body, and his legs swelled up.

The leaders of Canada would not fight the English. Ben and his friends headed back for Philadelphia.

Ben felt worse. It took five weeks for him to get better.

Leaders asked Ben to work on a committee to write the Declaration of Independence. Thomas Jefferson wrote the first version. Then John Adams and Ben made changes. Finally their job was done. The colonies voted to accept the Declaration of Independence on July 4, 1776. America was at war with England.

Ben and the other leaders were worried. The army needed guns. America didn't make guns. Without enough guns, they would lose the war.

They decided to send some men to France to ask for help. Ben was old and sick. But the leaders thought Ben was the best person to send. People in France saw Ben as a hero.

Benjamin Franklin, Thomas Jefferson, John Adams, Robert Livingston, and Roger Sherman wrote and revised the Declaration of Independence.

On October 29, 1776, Ben left on a ship for France. The trip was hard. Ben was glad the trip didn't take long. The crew gave him chicken to eat but it was too tough to chew. He had to eat dried salted beef. The food made his skin worse. He had sores all over his body. He even had sores under his hair. Ben felt terrible.

When they landed in France, Ben took a carriage to the city of Nantes. The driver stopped just before the road went through a dark woods. He told Ben that a gang of 18 robbers had killed people at that spot just two weeks earlier. Ben was thankful when they made it to Nantes safely.

Ben rested for a few days. Then he went to Paris. He knew that a lot of business was done at dinner parties. Ben held many parties. He charmed everyone. He loved playing party tricks. One of his favorite tricks was to wave his cane over rough water in a lake. The water became very calm. It seemed like magic to the other guests. Ben's magic trick was based on science.

The fashionable people at the court of France were fascinated by Ben. The people seated on the right are Marie Antoinette and Louis XVI.

Oil smoothed rough water. His cane had a hollow space to store oil. He opened the space before waving the cane over the water. The oil fell onto the water and made it smooth.

People wore formal clothes to parties. But Ben often wore the rough clothes of a **frontiersman** with the fur hat from the awful trip to Canada. People loved his clothes. Some ladies even started wearing wigs in the shape of Ben's

As ambassador to France, Ben negotiated treaties so the French would support the U.S. against Britain.

hat. Everyone bought pictures of Ben. His face was put on rings, bracelets, hats, and coats.

Ben thought all this fuss over him was funny. But he knew it could help America. And it did. Many French people gave money and guns to America.

In October 1777 the Americans won a big battle over the British. Ben was very happy. The battle might convince the French government to help America. Late that winter, the French king signed treaties with America. The French would fight the British.

The war went on for four more years. Sometimes it looked like the British would win. Other times it looked like the Americans would win. Whether the news was good or bad, Ben kept working for America.

Ben was in great pain. He had **gout**, a disease that made his foot and leg hurt so much that he often couldn't walk.

In November 1781 Ben got very good news. The Americans had beaten the British at the Battle of Yorktown. England had lost the war. Now Ben would write a peace treaty.

It took two years to work out a peace treaty with the English. Then Ben stayed in Paris. He spoke to other countries about America.

Finally, in 1785, Ben learned that he could go home. He had lived in Paris for nine years. He was very sad to leave his French friends. But Ben was excited to see his home again.

Ben's ship first went to England. He met his son, William, for the first time in more than ten years. William had stayed loyal to the king. He had spent time in prison. Ben and William still disagreed about the war. They didn't like each other very much.

Ben was busy as the ship sailed to America. He worked on a story about his life. A huge crowd of people welcomed Ben home. Everyone wanted to meet Ben.

The new United States didn't have rules to live by. It needed its own government. Leaders asked Ben to help write the **Constitution** and people came from every state except Rhode Island to take part in writing it. The meetings took place in Philadelphia, beginning in May 1787.

Ben went to almost every meeting. He listened to people talk. In June a big argument started. No one could agree on how the states would be represented in the new government. Some people wanted the number of **representatives** to be based on how many people lived in each state. Larger states would have more representatives. Other people wanted each state to have the same number of representatives.

The argument got very bad. People were afraid that the United States would fall apart. If they couldn't agree on what kind of government to have, how could the country work?

Finally Ben told everyone they needed to work things out. People listened to the 81-year-old man. They set up a special committee, which worked hard for two months. Then it was time to vote on the Constitution.

Ben wanted to give a speech. He wrote down the words to say. But his leg hurt too much to stand up. A friend read the speech for Ben. He asked the delegates to vote for the Constitution even if they didn't agree with everything in it. They took his advice. The Constitution passed.

During the next two years, Ben worked on the story of his life. He also wrote an article against slavery. He was in a lot of pain, and most of the

The Constitution of the United States was signed in 1787. Here George Washington is shown holding a copy of this important document. Ben is seen sitting second from the left.

time he had to stay in bed. But that didn't slow Ben. When Ben didn't have the strength to write, his grandson wrote down his words for him. He had many visitors. He still told jokes.

On April 17, 1790, Ben Franklin died. He was 84 years old. The city of Philadelphia held a huge funeral to honor him.

Ben was remembered for many things. He helped America change from a group of colonies to a young nation. He helped form America's government. He invented a stove, lightning rods, and other useful things. He discovered more about electricity. He shared his wisdom in the book he wrote about his life. Ben tried to make the world a better place. Because he succeeded, he was a great leader.

GLOSSARY

almanac a book that has a calendar and tells about the weather for the next year

apprentice a child who works for someone while learning that person's job

cargo the things carried on a ship

colonies a group of people living together in a new land and tied by law to their old country

constitution the basic laws of a nation

critic a person who finds fault

eclipse a short time when the sun or moon looks dark because it is hidden by the earth's shadow

experiment a test to prove whether an idea is correct

frontiersman a person who lives on land that hasn't been settled by other people

gout a disease that makes the foot swell and hurt a lot

harbor deep water next to the land where ships can anchor safely

militia a group of people who fight for a country in an emergency

representative a person who speaks and acts for everyone in a larger group

smallpox a disease with fever and sores that killed many people

treaty an agreement between two nations

CHRONOLOGY

1706 Benjamin Franklin born in Boston on January 17

1718 Apprenticed to his older brother, James, owner of a printing shop

1723 Runs away to Philadelphia; begins working as a printer for Samuel Keimer

1728 Opens printing shop with Hugh Meredith

1730 Marries Deborah Read on September 1

1732 Publishes first edition of *Poor Richard's Almanac* on December 19

1747 Begins writing about his experiments with electricity

1751 Becomes deputy postmaster general of North America

1757   Travels to London to act for Pennsylvania and settle disputes with the Penn family

1765   Works to end the Stamp Act

1775   Deborah Read Franklin dies; Ben returns to America

1776   Works on the Declaration of Independence; travels to France to get guns and money for America

1782   Works on a peace treaty with England

1785   Returns to Philadelphia

1787   Helps create the Constitution

1790   Benjamin Franklin dies quietly at his home on April 17

COLONIAL TIME LINE

1607 Jamestown, Virginia, is settled by the English.

1620 Pilgrims on the Mayflower land at Plymouth, Massachusetts.

1623 The Dutch settle New Netherlands, the colony that later becomes New York.

1630 Massachusetts Bay Colony is started.

1634 Maryland is settled as a Roman Catholic colony. Later Maryland becomes a safe place for people with different religious beliefs.

1636 Roger Williams is thrown out of the Massachusetts Bay Colony. He settles Rhode Island, the first colony to give people freedom of religion.

1682 William Penn forms the colony of Pennsylvania.

1688 Pennsylvania Quakers make the first formal protest against slavery.

1692 Trials for witchcraft are held in Salem, Massachusetts.

1712 Slaves revolt in New York. Twenty-one blacks are killed as punishment.

1720 Major smallpox outbreak occurs in Boston. Cotton Mather and some doctors try a new treatment. Many people think the new treatment shouldn't be used.

1754 French and Indian War begins. It ends nine years later.

1761 Benjamin Banneker builds a wooden clock that keeps precise time.

1765 Britain passes the Stamp Act. Violent protests break out in the colonies. The Stamp Act is ended the next year.

1775 The battles of Lexington and Concord begin the American Revolution.

1776 Declaration of Independence is signed.

FURTHER READING

Adler, David A. *Benjamin Franklin: Printer, Inventor, Statesman.* New York: Holiday House, 1992.

——. *A Picture Book of Benjamin Franklin.* New York: Holiday House, 1990.

Birch, Beverley. *Benjamin Franklin's Adventures with Electricity.* Science Stories Series. Robin Bell Corfield, contributor. New York: Barrons Juveniles, 1996.

Fleming, Candace. *The Hatmaker's Sign: A Story by Benjamin Franklin.* New York: Orchard Books, 1998.

Rudy, Lisa Jo, ed. *The Ben Franklin Book of Easy and Incredible Experiments.* Franklin Institute, contributor. New York: John Wiley & Sons, 1995.

INDEX

INDEX

PICTURE CREDITS

ABOUT THE AUTHORS ═══════

BRUCE and BECKY DUROST FISH are freelance writers and editors who have worked on more than 100 books for children and young adults. They have degrees in history and literature and live in the high desert of Central Oregon.

Senior Consulting Editor **ARTHUR M. SCHLESINGER, JR.** is the leading American historian of our time. He won the Pulitzer prize for his book *The Age of Jackson* (1945) and again for *A Thousand Days* (1965). His chronicle of the Kennedy Administration also won a National Book Award. He has written many other books including a multi-volume series, *The Age of Roosevelt*. Professor Schlesinger is the Albert Schweitzer Professor of the Humanities at the City University of New York, and has been involved in several other Chelsea House projects, including the *Revolutionary War Leaders* biographies on the most prominent figures of early American history.